D1247441

Scottish Alphabet

Scottish Alphabet

By Rickey E. Pittman

Illustrated by Connie McLennan

PELICAN PUBLISHING COMPANY

GRETNA 2008

To the children of Scotland, wherever God has placed you.
Slàinte mhath *(good health)!*

*The word "Pelican" and the depiction of a pelican are trademarks
of Pelican Publishing Company, Inc., and are registered in the
U.S. Patent and Trademark Office.*

Library of Congress Cataloging-in-Publication Data

Pittman, Rickey.
  Scottish alphabet / by Rickey E. Pittman ; Illustrated by Connie McLennan.
    p. cm.
  ISBN-13: 978-1-58980-596-5 (alk. paper) 1. Alphabet—Juvenile poetry.
2. Scotland—Juvenile poetry. 3. Children's poetry, American. I. McLennan, Connie,
ill. II. Title.
  PS3566.I8532S36 2008
  811'.54—dc22

                              2008007317

Printed in Korea
Published by Pelican Publishing Company, Inc.
1000 Burmaster Street, Gretna, Louisiana 70053

November
30

St. Andrew's Day

A is for St. Andrew's Day,
A day of dance and song.
Go to the *ceilidh* with me,
Oh, won't you come along?

B is for the bagpipes,
With melodies so sweet.
See the soldiers' stately steps
As the pipers march the streets.

C is for the **caber**
Tossed in the Highland Games,
And for Scottish castles,
Where once lived men of fame.

D is for the daggers
Of the Highlanders so bold,
And also dirks and **sgian dubh**,
Impressive to behold.

E is for Edinburgh,
The ancient Scottish town.
I hope you visit there one day
And walk its sacred ground.

F is for the **Highland fling.**
See them dance,
Hear them sing!

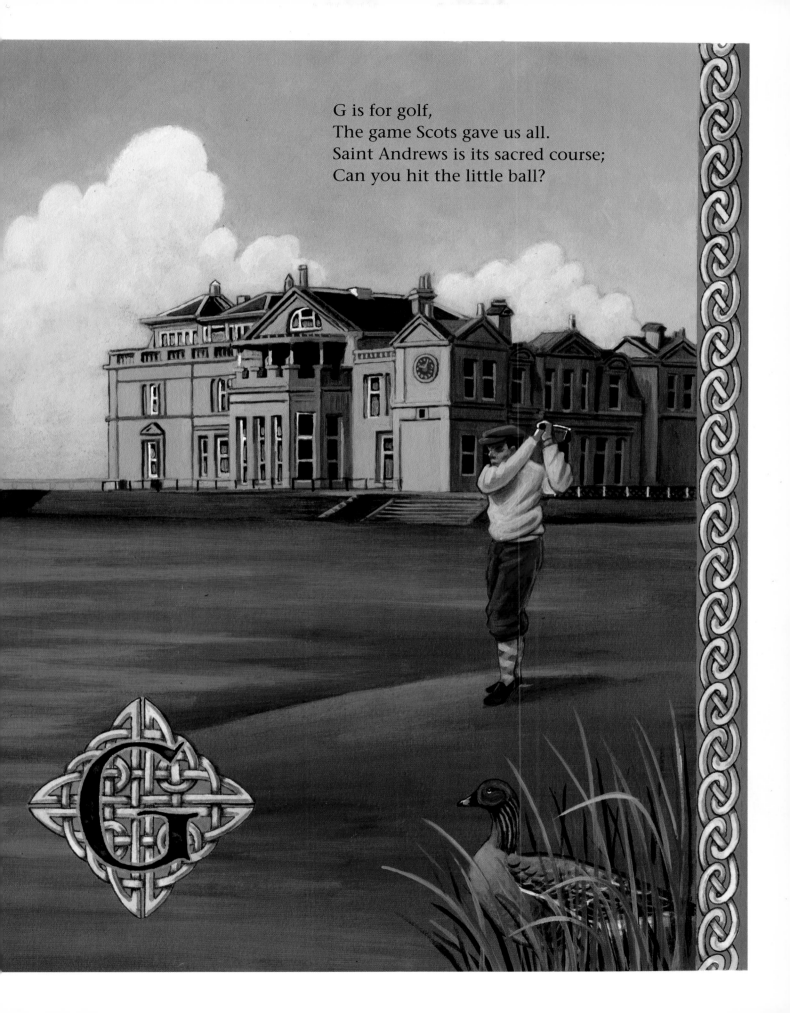

G is for golf,
The game Scots gave us all.
Saint Andrews is its sacred course;
Can you hit the little ball?

H is for the Highlanders,
Who loved the **haggis** so.
They lived up in the mountains
And hunted in the snow.

Iona

I is for Iona,
Where ancient kings now rest.
Their stories are our history,
And by that we are blessed.

J is for the Jacobites,
Bonnie Prince Charlie's men.
They wore blue bonnets on
    their heads
And fought on hill and glen.

K is for the woolen kilt
That Scottish men do wear.
Each clan has its own tartan,
Woven at Dundee with care.

L is for Lomond,
A famous Scottish **loch**.
Lads and lassies walk its shores
To hold sweet hands and talk.

M is for the martyrs' stones,
Scattered across our land.
Cairns piled high in memory
Remind us of each man.

N is for Nessie,
Our monster in Loch Ness.
See her swim so skillfully
And stretch her long, long neck.

O is for the field of oats
Giving strength to a Scottish **bairn**,
Used in bread and porridge,
And the cookies in your hand.

P is for **peat**
That we dig from the bog.
Toss it in the fire;
It burns like a log.

Q is for the Scottish queen
Upon her throne so royal.
She is Mary, Queen of Scots.
Her subjects were truly loyal.

R is for Robert,
The Bruce, as he was known,
Beloved and fearless leader,
Crowned king of Scots at Scone.

S is for Shetland,
That wild island pony,
For the **sporran** the Highlanders wear,
And also for Scotch whisky.

T is for the thistle,
Scotland's national flower.
I love to see its purple blooms,
But I fear its prickly power!

Scotland

Shetland Islands

Northern Ireland

England

Wales

Atlantic Ocean

U is for the United Kingdom,
Four countries which are one:
England, Wales, and Scotland,
And of course, Northern Ireland.

V is for the victory
Scots won at Bannockburn.
England's Edward learned a lesson,
So home he did return.

W is for William Wallace,
A brave heart he had shown,
Defeating the English at Stirling Bridge,
For Scotland was his home!

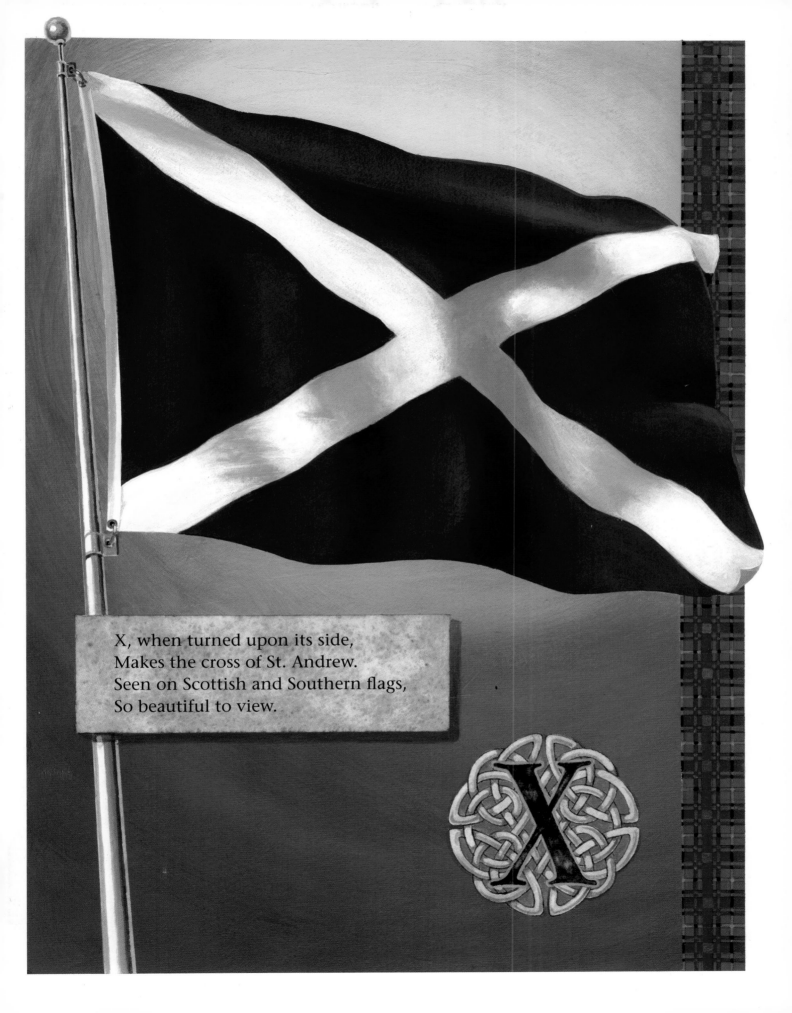

X, when turned upon its side,
Makes the cross of St. Andrew.
Seen on Scottish and Southern flags,
So beautiful to view.

Y is for **yowe,**
A Scottish word for ewe.
We weave her wool into tartan cloth
Of red, green, black, or blue.

Z is for **Zetland**,
Or Shetland as it's known,
Famous for puffins and fiddlers,
And **brochs** and standing stones.

Scottish Glossary

bairn—a child

broch—type of circular hollow-walled stone tower found only in Scotland. They were built without mortar.

caber—twenty-foot-long pole that weighs about 120 pounds. It was thrown as a show of strength.

cairns—pile of stones that serves as a marker or monument

ceilidh (pronounced KAY-lee or KALE-ee)—social gathering or dinner where people sing, dance, and tell stories

haggis—seasoned pudding made of animal organs

Highland fling—a lively dance from the Scottish Highlands

loch—Scottish word for lake

peat—vegetation, usually moss, that is dried for use as a fuel

sgian dubh (pronounced SKEE-AN-DOO)—a short-bladed knife with a black hilt, which the Highlanders wore at the outside top of the right sock. Also spelled skean-dhu.

sporran (pronounced SPOOR-run)—pouch made of fur or leather worn hanging from a belt in front of a High-lander's kilt

St. Andrew—patron saint of Scotland. He was the brother of St. Peter. Scotland celebrates this saint on November 30 each year.

yowe—Scottish word for ewe. Rhymes with "now."

Zetland—formerly the official name for the Shetland Islands